MW00884471

IN EVERY LIFE

IN EVERY LIFE: 50 REFLECTIONS

Blog Posts from 2015-2016

AMY EKEH

The majority of the Scripture quotations contained herein are from the New Revised Standard Version Bible, copyright © 1989 by the Division of Christian Education of the National Council of the Churches of Christ in the U.S.A., and are used by permission. All rights reserved.

Cover design by John Vineyard.

These reflections originally appeared at amyekeh.com/blog.

In Every Life: 50 Reflections
Copyright © 2017, Amy Ekeh

Dedicated to Fr. Tim Church.

In liturgy, in words, in friendship,
he taught me that life is the moment of salvation.

*"What draws people to be friends is that
they see the same truth. They share it."*

-- C.S. Lewis

INTRODUCTION

Last night at 2:00 a.m., my six-year-old son tapped my husband on the shoulder, and my four-year-old son tapped me on the shoulder. That gentle yet insistent tap means "let me into the bed, please." My husband dutifully got up and gave the six-year-old his spot. I opened my eyes long enough to lift my four-year-old into bed next to me. I held him for a while, and then turned my back to get into a more comfortable position.

After a few minutes I heard sniffles. I looked over and my little one was wiping his eyes on his sleeve. "What's wrong?" I asked him. He blinked hard and swallowed. "I'm lonely!" he said, more tears streaming down his face. There he lay, nestled in between his big brother and his mom in the comfiest, fluffiest bed in the house, and he was lonely! What he meant was that he wanted my arms around him.

Our own cries of "I'm lonely!" do not go unheeded. Although it does not always feel like God's arms are around us, our faith tells us that they are. But sometimes we need to be reminded. We need someone else who believes it to tell us. We need to be encouraged to believe that he is there, right beside us, dwelling in us, breathing with us, enlivening us, *intimately* present: "I am in my Father, and you in me, and I in you" (John 14:20).

I have depended upon those reassuring voices in my own life, those reminders that God is present, that he holds us in a warm embrace of freedom and love.

Yes, in every life, rains will fall and fires will burn. In every life, there will be confusion and times of deep, intense questioning. In every life, in the middle of winter when the nights are long and we are awakened by the cold, we will ask if God is there. For a while we may only hear silence. But then something or someone will remind us that God *is* present.

In every life.

Amy Ekeh
February 2017

MY SALVATION

Those who have met me in recent years may be surprised to know that I was a somewhat melancholic teen. For years I saw the world as very black and white; I saw good and bad. I wanted everything to be good, and I was unhappy that some things were bad. Despite my own happy childhood I looked around at the world and saw what I considered to be a negative place. I couldn't figure out how I fit into it or how it could ever feel "right."

I remember a conversation I had with the man who mentored me through those teen years and many years beyond – a parish priest who put up with my melancholy and who succeeded in the careful balancing act of loving me just as I was, while simultaneously bringing about a substantial change in me. One day I told him just how bad this life is, just how miserable. I was armed with a quote from St. Teresa of Avila that I thought captured the whole awful mess of life. "Life," I said, "is like a bad night in a bad inn."

I was sure that God and all his angels and saints agreed with me. But Fr. Tim didn't. He didn't agree with me at all. And his response shifted the entire worldview going on in my teenage brain. It changed the way I saw everything including myself, him, God, suffering, my future. It changed the way I saw my world and how I fit into it. Fr. Tim told me that life isn't a bad night in a bad inn. "Life," he said, "is the moment of your salvation."

I have never stopped believing that. I have never stopped seeing my world and my life from this fuller perspective – one that recognizes life as a gracious moment, a time of encounters and relationships that bring me closer and closer to the heart of God if only I will allow it. Sure, sometimes the inn feels run down or drafty or even dangerous. Sometimes the other people in the inn rob, cheat and steal – or gossip or disappoint or annoy me. Sometimes it is dark and the night in the inn feels long. But the moment of my salvation is long, long enough for me to settle into the beauty of this inn and its people, long enough to learn how to live here with them and with myself, long enough to grow into my own salvation.

God has not left me here to flounder until morning comes. He lives with me here, in this time and place. This is the moment of my salvation.

* * *

LESSONS OF THE TREES:
UNDER THE FIG TREE

Nathanael said to him, "How do you know me?"
Jesus answered, "I saw you under the fig tree."
John 1:48

Have you ever been noticed across a crowded room? Has anyone ever paid attention to you unexpectedly? Has someone noticed something special about you – something small or something you didn't think anyone knew, or something you didn't even know yourself? Has anyone ever looked at you in such a way that pages of words and thoughts were communicated in a single moment?

And how did that make you feel? How did *being connected* with that person make you feel? Alive? Like the best version of yourself? Not alone?

We live in a constant state of tension between two extreme opinions of ourselves. On the one hand we are utterly enamored with ourselves – this is the side of us that subconsciously thanks God that we are not like the rest of humanity (cf. Lk. 18:11). On the other hand, we doubt and even despise ourselves to the point of believing ourselves unlovable ("If they *really knew me,* they would not love me").

But what if there was someone whose gaze alone could penetrate us with such clarity that we moved away from this exaggerated tension into the peaceful middle, where we could see ourselves as we truly are – genuinely flawed but entirely lovable? What if there was someone whose gaze expressed such love to us that we believed once and for all that *we are the beloved?* What if there was someone who could simply say "I saw you" – and in those words communicate to us that he knows all the little things about us, all the special things, all the things no one else ever noticed before? How would we respond to that remarkable person?

Nathanael responded: "Rabbi, you are the Son of God; you are the King of Israel" (Jn. 1:49). And then he followed him.

I suppose one who noticed us across a crowded room and loved us so would be irresistible. I suppose that is what Nathanael felt. Jesus saw Nathanael – saw him, knew him, and loved him. And as one of his disciples, he taught him, nurtured him, challenged him, called him friend, encouraged him and died for him. He made promises to him, and he kept those promises. Then he went and prepared a place for him.

Under the fig tree, you too have been seen. Loved, taught, nurtured and befriended. Everything about you. Seen, known and loved beneath the fig tree.

"Standing before him with open hearts, letting him look at us, we see that gaze of love which Nathanael glimpsed on the day when Jesus said to him: 'I saw you under the fig tree' (Jn. 1:48)" (Pope Francis, Evangelii Gaudium 264).

* * *

IN EVERY LIFE

"I have a dogmatic certainty:
God is in every person's life.
God is in everyone's life.
Even if the life of a person has been a disaster,
even if it is destroyed by vices, drugs
or anything else – God is in this person's life.
You can, you must try to seek God
in every human life."

*Pope Francis,
Interview with America Magazine*

* * *

THE GOOD AND THE BAD
AT THE TABLE OF THE LORD

This year on the feast of Corpus Christi, I was struck by a line in the *Lauda Sion* sequence recited at Mass: *"Bad and good the feast are sharing."*

I've been thinking a lot lately about how God seems to have a preference for imperfect people. Read a few pages of Scripture and you discover a murderer was the greatest prophet of the Old Testament (Moses), and one who was at least complicit in murder was the greatest missionary of the New Testament (Paul). King David was an adulterer but also a man after God's own heart. Peter betrayed his best friend and his Lord but, in the eyes of that same Lord, he was a Rock.

Bad and good this feast are sharing – this Eucharistic feast, this feast of life, feast of divine love that seeps in and around us. If we had to be "good" before we could come to the feast, what would be the point? It is this feast that can heal the bad in all of us.

When it comes to human beings, it seems that God prefers transformation to perfection. This is what his friendship and his table are all about: *"Very bread, good shepherd, tend us, Jesus, of your love befriend us, You refresh us, you defend us, Your eternal goodness send us in the land of life to see."*

ADVICE FROM A BOXER

I don't typically get my spiritual advice from professional boxers. But one day while driving I happened to hear part of an interview of pro boxer George Foreman (yes, the one who named all five of his sons "George"). With a stereotypical idea of what boxers are like, I was caught off guard by something he said. Actually "caught off guard" doesn't really do it justice. I was quite touched!

Foreman was talking about his estranged relationship with his father, who was an alcoholic. He said that one day he looked at his father and asked himself, "Do I want to have a father or not?" He realized his choice was to either forgive his father or just be without. So he decided to forgive him even though it was very, very hard. Foreman went on to say that forgiveness is the greatest of life's lessons, an indispensable life skill. Without forgiveness, he said, there are no relationships.

If I had heard this sentiment during a homily, I probably would have mildly appreciated it and gone on with my life. But coming from George Foreman, I admit it, I was deeply impacted. *There are no relationships without forgiveness.* At least no meaningful ones.

Forgiveness is one of those spiritual arts that is best learned at home, in the family. Goodness knows we have many occasions there to practice! If we don't learn forgiveness at home, it can be very difficult to learn it in the world; and if we don't learn it young, it can be much harder to learn it later in life. That being said, it is never too late to learn or practice this life skill. So break out that George Foreman Grill (you know you have one) and gather the family around. Have a burger or a panini and celebrate the art of forgiveness!

Post Script: I just read up on George Foreman and discovered two very important pieces of information. First, he is a native Texan. Second, he is an ordained minister! I also found an interview in which he was asked if there could be any circumstance in which he would not be able to forgive someone. His response: "Oh, not in this life now. I've found my peace of mind. If you wake up one morning without forgiveness in your heart, you'll wake up without children, without a husband, without a wife. Forgiveness is the only way that you can bind love and friendship. Without it, you are empty." Preach it, George!

* * *

"PRAISED BY HAPPY VOICES"

Maybe it's the Texas girl in me, but I'm finding peace in these long summer evenings. It's just the right time of year to share with you one of my favorite evening prayers, a lingering companion from my Episcopal days. I remember so clearly the little chapel at Holy Nativity Church in Plano, Texas, where we used to say this prayer together in the evenings.

The *Phos Hilaron* is an ancient Christian hymn and one of the oldest we have outside of the New Testament. (Several New Testament writers incorporate hymns or hymn fragments into their work, such as the familiar hymn of the self-emptying of Jesus included by Paul in his letter to the Philippians; see Phil. 2:6-11.)

We don't know who wrote this lovely prayer, but we do know it has been around since at least the 3rd century. St. Basil, writing in the 4th century, referred to the *Phos Hilaron* as an already cherished prayer of the Church.

The hymn, which refers to the *vesper* (or *evening*) light, was sung at the lighting of lamps at dusk, a joyful testament to the light of the world.

Phos Hilaron

O gracious Light,
pure brightness of the everliving Father in heaven,
O Jesus Christ, holy and blessed!

Now as we come to the setting of the sun,
and our eyes behold the vesper light,
we sing your praises, O God:
Father, Son, and Holy Spirit.

You are worthy at all times to be praised
by happy voices,
O Son of God, O Giver of life,
and to be glorified through all the worlds.

* * *

THE PROLONGATION OF THE INCARNATION

Pope Francis' document "The Joy of the Gospel" *(Evangelii Gaudium)* is not a dense theological read. It is typically Francis – straightforward, often informal, and always calling us to something higher. The document is peppered with what you might call "Francis phrases" – striking phrases that tell a truth and leave an impression. One of my favorites is Francis' reference to "the unruly freedom of the Word" (*EG* 22). That simple phrase captures the living nature of God's Word: the inspiration that breathes life into it, the way it has its own movement and mission, and how it should not be and *cannot be* controlled by human beings – not even in their own well-meaning interpretations and applications. We must accept that God's Word "accomplishes what it wills in ways that surpass our calculations and ways of thinking" (*EG* 22).

Another of my favorite phrases from the document is *"the prolongation of the incarnation"* (*EG* 179). First of all, it has a nice ring to it! It rhymes just as nicely in Spanish (which I would imagine is the language Pope Francis was "thinking in") as it does in English: *la prolongación de la encarnación.*

So what is the "prolongation of the incarnation"? What does this poetic phrase mean? Francis writes:

"God's word teaches that our brothers and sisters are the prolongation of the incarnation for each of us: 'As you did it to one of these, the least of my brethren, you did it to me' (Mt. 25:40)" (*EG* 179).   Pope Francis makes the point – and makes it crystal clear – that the Gospel message has implications for how we treat each other.   The "prolongation of the incarnation" simply means that Christ lives in every human being. That is one way he continues to be incarnate, continues to be with us. Therefore if we claim to love *him*, we must love *them*.

This is not a new idea, of course. It is an ancient idea. In addition to the words of Christ himself, I think of St. John, who the stories say told his own little flock to "love one another" so many times that his disciples got annoyed and asked him why he kept saying it. He answered, "If you do this, it is enough." He did not say this because it didn't matter if they loved *God* or not, but because in loving one another, they were loving God very well. John also wrote, "Those who say, 'I love God,' and hate their brothers or sisters, are liars; for those who do not love a brother or sister whom they have seen, cannot love God whom they have not seen" (1 Jn. 4:20). That's another crystal clear way of saying: when you love your brothers and sisters, you prolong the incarnation!

* * *

THE "GOD IS IN CONTROL" CHURCH

I used to live in a strange town called Waldorf. The first time I ever went to Waldorf was to eat lunch with two new colleagues from my first parish job. Carol directed me to the restaurant by telling me to drive south into Waldorf, then turn left on "Mattawoman-Beantown Road." Then Cheryl mentioned a helpful landmark: "You'll see a giant paint can on the left side of the road right before your turn. The giant paint can is how we mark things in Waldorf. Everything is either before or after the paint can."

I found the whole thing very strange. Waldorf was always like that for me, though I did become quite accustomed to saying "Mattawoman-Beantown" and giving directions by orienting everything around a very large paint can that was perched on top of a strip mall.

After slogging through seven or eight years of purgatorial Waldorfian living, I was informed by my sister-in-law's Swiss boyfriend that Waldorf means "wooded village" in German. It sounded so lovely! If only!

But I shouldn't complain. Waldorf had its charms. And one of them was a little non-denominational church situated on Waldorf's main thoroughfare, nestled into one of Waldorf's most nondescript strip malls. It was called the "God Is In Control Church."

Now that is a great name for a church. Sure, we Catholics have very fine church names: Holy Infant, Our Lady Help of Christians, Prince of Peace, The Basilica of the National Shrine of the Immaculate Conception. We have churches named for wonderful saints, devotions and mysteries. But I think Waldorf may have one-upped us this time. Every time I drove past that little storefront church, I felt great about life. I might have been living in a strange town, surrounded by suburbia, yearning for a wooded village. But God was in control. God was in control. And that was enough.

Yes, the members of that little church had done something right. Just by choosing a name and hanging up a sign, they were evangelizing me. The "God Is In Control Church" made me happy. It made me feel safe. It made me want to nod my head and shout "Amen!"

Plus, it was *almost* as much fun to say as "Mattawoman-Beantown."

* * *

THE SACRED DYNAMIC OF FRANK CONVERSATION

Last Sunday the Gospel reading was the familiar story of Martha and Mary (Luke 10:38-42). As the reading began, I wasn't expecting to hear anything new. I know this one; I know the words of Jesus; I know the lesson.

But I was blessed to be surprised. I was surprised by the words of Martha. Not because she sounded distressed, or frustrated, or annoyed with her sister. I wasn't surprised by her resentment or even her logic.

I was surprised by how bold she was with Jesus, how frank, how confident.

Thinking back over the Gospels, there were many people who were quite deferential toward Jesus. They spoke and acted with fitting respect for the masterful teacher and wonder-worker he was. But there were others who were surprisingly informal with Jesus. Perfect strangers approached him – they asked him for things, they touched him, they laid their heaviest burdens on him. Indeed, many who approached Jesus did not just ask; they commanded! Remember Jairus: "My daughter is at the point of death. Come and lay your hands on her" (Mk. 5:23) or Bartimaeus of Jericho: "Let me see again" (Mk. 10:51).

Martha's command was just as direct: "Tell her to help me."

Certainly the presence of Jesus made people take notice. There was charisma, authority and even power over the natural world. But apparently he was not intimidating. There was something about his presence that drew people close, unmasking them and inviting frank conversation and bold requests.

Now of course, when we are frank and bold with Jesus, he may be frank and bold with us. Martha may not have liked Jesus' gentle rebuke. But John's Gospel tells us that Jesus loved her (Jn. 11:5), and she certainly knew that. There was no need for Martha to hide her heart from Jesus. The honesty, the unmasking, is what allowed Jesus to penetrate that heart, to love it and transform it. This is the power of honest prayer, the sacred dynamic of frank conversation.

* * *

FEISTY CHILDREN

As I write this post, my four-year-old son is sitting in "time out" because he disobeyed Mom. From his perspective, I am not being nice. But from my perspective, this restrictive act (temporarily curtailing his freedom), is slowly setting my son free. He is learning by cause and effect what is acceptable behavior in relationships so that once he is "full-grown," he will make good use of all that free will.

Would you agree that Julian's perspective right now is immature and incomplete? Would you agree that he can trust me, that I have his best interest at heart? Would you agree that I want nothing more than his happiness and that I yearn for a strong, healthy and loving relationship with him when he is an adult (which is a much longer-term situation than how he feels about me tonight)? Would you agree that what he is experiencing now is less like *punishment* and more like . . . *"molding clay"* (cf. Jer. 19:1-11)?

Think of yourself as a feisty four-year-old whose loving parent wants nothing more than your happiness, your freedom, and ultimately, your love. Think of God patiently waiting for you to grow in maturity and wisdom – loving you, teaching you and nourishing you along the way.

These words from the prophet Hosea tell it perfectly. They tell of the parent whose "bands of love" are not always recognized as kindness by the sometimes rebellious, always beloved, child:

When Israel was a child, I loved him,
and out of Egypt I called my son.
The more I called them,
the more they went from me;
they kept sacrificing to [false gods],
and offering incense to idols.
Yet it was I who taught Ephraim to walk,
I took them up in my arms;
but they did not know that I healed them.
I led them with cords of human kindness,
with bands of love.
I was to them like those
who lift infants to their cheeks.
I bent down to them and fed them.

Hosea 11:1-4

* * *

A DEFINITION OF PRAYER

I like to begin classes on prayer by asking participants: "What is prayer?" I don't do this because I'm fishing for a particular answer. I do it because I want to hear – and I want them to hear – the variety and the depth of one another's answers. I have never heard a *wrong* answer to this question, but I have heard some quite beautiful ones. They are all based on the genuine experience and the spiritual personalities of the folks giving the answers.

One of my favorite "definitions" of prayer was written by Servant of God Catherine Doherty in her typical down-to-earth and straight-to-the-heart style. It captures both the stillness and the movement of prayer, the way prayer can be both vibrant conversation and quiet being. As Catherine knew very well, sometimes prayer is just being in a meaningful moment with the One you love. It is a meeting of two loves.

"How can you define prayer, except by saying that it is love? It is love expressed in speech, and love expressed in silence. To put it another way, prayer is the meeting of two loves: the love of God and our love. That's all there is to prayer."

– Servant of God Catherine Doherty,
Soul of My Soul: Reflections from a Life of Prayer

GOD, WHY DO YOU HAVE TO BE SO MYSTERIOUS?

While studying the account of Moses and the Burning Bush in her religious education textbook, my daughter got a little bit irritated with God. She felt he was being intentionally difficult when it came to naming himself. "Why not just give a name? What's with *'I am who I am'*?" (Ex. 3:14)

It's a fair enough question. I didn't say much in response, but I did point out that it would be a little bit disappointing if God said, "Hello, my name is Bob." Bob is a great name, but it isn't the least bit mysterious.

Sometimes it may seem like God is being difficult on purpose. But he's probably just being himself. He's being mysterious. He's being "I am." I experience this Difficult Mystery when I teach Scripture. Sometimes I feel like I'm entering a world where I don't belong. I start to understand it, and then I suddenly stop. I come close to something and then it unravels into a hundred other things. Why is it this way? And how can I take other people to a place that is so far beyond me?

But that's just the privilege of knowing God. How boring would it be to have a God who can only take us places we've already been, or tell us things we already know? No, I prefer a God whose name I don't understand, whose Book changes every time I pick it up, whose ways are not my ways, who takes me places I've never been, and who tells me things I never knew.

Why does God have to be so mysterious? Because *he is!*

* * *

GOOD OLD-FASHIONED ZINGER

"If you believe what you like in the gospels,
and reject what you don't like,
it is not the gospel you believe, but yourself."

St. Augustine

* * *

REPENTANCE VS. GUILT

*"Godly grief produces a repentance that leads
to salvation and brings no regret, but worldly
grief produces death" (2 Cor. 7:10).*

This verse from the rich book of 2 Corinthians tells us
all we need to know about the difference between *guilt*
and *repentance*. This is an important distinction to
make. It has extreme consequences for our spiritual
lives, for the way we relate to God and the way we
believe he relates to us.

Paul coins the term "Godly grief," and he contrasts it
with what we might call plain old guilt. There are
several things to know about Godly grief: 1) It
produces "repentance," a term that in Scripture is
associated with a change of mind and heart, a real
conversion or turning. 2) This repentance, or change
of heart, leads to salvation. Why? Because when we
recognize and turn away from sin, we turn back to
God. 3) It "brings no regret." This is my favorite part.
Godly grief leads to repentance, which turns us to our
Savior, who frees us in mind and body. When we turn
to him with contrite hearts, the slate is wiped clean.
Life with no regret? That sounds awesome!

"Worldly grief" is less complicated. It just produces
death. Worldly grief (guilt) is the kind of sorrow and
fretting that focuses on ourselves – what I did wrong,

how bad I am, why I can't stop. The reason this kind of grief gets us nowhere is that it has no point of reference beyond ourselves. It turns inward and stagnates.

Feeling bad for doing something wrong is a natural human emotion. It brings us to a fork in the road. In one direction, we can choose an open and honest sorrow for sin that unites us with a merciful God and reconciles us with our brothers and sisters (who are also sinners!). In this direction we move rather freely toward salvation, unfettered by regret and shame. In the other direction lies the dead end of guilt. If we follow this path, we get tripped up by our own roadblocks until we finally just stumble into a pit. In the pit we feel restricted. Trapped within ourselves, it is dark, and we lose all sense of direction. We experience the slow, numbing death of negativity and self-loathing. From the bottom of the pit, how could we think of a Savior when we can't stop thinking about ourselves? How can we hear *his* voice when we are so focused on the voices in our own heads?

So let's strive to cultivate Godly grief – not in order to be sad but as a way of being honest. This is how we articulate within ourselves a need for something beyond ourselves, a need for the one who saves. This is life instead of death. This is life without regret.

* * *

IS PETITIONARY PRAYER CHILDISH?

A very dear friend of mine, and one much older and wiser than me, once told me that she had been praying to God to help her find a used car. She had something very particular in mind, and she had found exactly the right thing, except that it cost $500 too much. "But that's my fault," she said. "I forgot to tell God my budget." At the time, I thought she was being silly and simplistic. But in truth, Maria was light years ahead of me when it comes to prayer. Maria is what you might call a *friend of God.* I should be sitting at her feet, saying as the disciples said to Jesus, "Teach me to pray."

We may think it is naïve and unsophisticated to ask God for specific things. He already knows what we want, so why waste the time and mental energy? Isn't our prayer time better spent in adoration or contemplation? And if we're really being honest, aren't we afraid that we will doubt or even resent God if we ask for "specifics" and then don't get them? Petitionary prayer, it seems, can lead us into an intellectual quagmire of questions, objections and pitfalls.

That's why Maria and those like her have so much to teach us. As much as I may have wondered at Maria's "brand" of faith, I deeply admired her. The simplicity of her prayer was not born of simplicity of mind.

Maria was clever, uncommonly clever. Rather, the simplicity of Maria's prayer came from the simplicity of her heart, a heart that was focused like a laser on one thing: God's magnificent providence. The way Maria saw things, God was both utterly transcendent and entirely involved in her life. He was the One Seated on the Throne and the one who was right beside her. He was the One in whom we live and move and have our being, and he was the one who would help her purchase just the right used car.

Maria did not waste her time with intellectual questions about petitionary prayer. Instead, she followed the command of Christ and asked God for every little thing (Mt. 7:7-11). And how did God respond to Maria? Not by answering each prayer with a miracle (though he did do amazing things for her!). But he responded by being her lifelong companion, her constant friend. He responded by giving her a peace that was the natural reward for her trust.

When I looked into Maria's eyes, I saw an ocean of calm and a confidence that took me aback. It was prayer that did this. Childlike? Perhaps. And to such as these belongs the Kingdom of God.

* * *

IF YOU CAN'T WASH THEIR FEET, HOW WILL YOU DIE FOR THEM?

The first chapter of John's Gospel introduces Jesus as the *logos* (Greek for "the Word"). A *word* communicates something; Jesus is what God wants to say to the world. In fact, New Testament scholar Francis Moloney loosely translates John 1:18 as: "He [Jesus] has told God's story."

As the divine *logos,* not only Jesus' words but everything he does expresses something to us about God. Jesus is not just a *messenger* of God's words; he *is* God's self-expression.

John is the only Gospel that tells the story of Jesus washing the feet of the disciples at the Last Supper. In this unique story, the divine *logos* speaks loudly. John does not narrate the details of the meal or what we now call the institution of the Eucharist. Instead, he tells a simple story about Jesus with a basin of water and a towel, doing something we never expected. He washes the dirty feet of his friends.

Peter is appalled, remember? But Jesus is patient. He says to Peter, "What I am doing, you will not understand now. But you will understand later." When he is finished, he asks his friends, "Do you know what I have done for you? I have given you a model to follow."

The foot-washing is startling, and Jesus' command to imitate his humble deed asks a lot of us. But it is nothing compared to the Cross. Ultimately, this is where Jesus goes. This is where he says to us again, *"What I am doing, you will not understand now. But you will understand later."* This is where he asks us for the last time, *"Do you know what I have done for you? I have given you a model to follow."* This is where we hear the ultimate echo of John's testimony about Jesus: *"He loved his own in the world and he loved them to the end" (13:1).*

Now imagine your friends, imagine those who need you, and even imagine your enemies – those who have hurt you or failed you, those in your life who are most difficult to love, respect or care for. Now imagine that you take up a towel and a basin of water. You kneel down and carefully wash their feet, and gently dry them. You might not want to do it at first, although you know God has done it for you so many times. But if you can't wash the feet of every person in your life, how will you go to the Cross, how will you lay down your life for them, how will you love your own to the end?

Jesus has told God's story. And now we are his *logos,* his Word, his self-expression in the world. We have been given a model to follow. Will we do it?

* * *

"HE VANISHED"

The story of the appearance of the Risen Christ to the disciples on the road to Emmaus is well-known – perhaps *too* well-known! It's been used for so many meditations and lessons that you might actually think you're tired of hearing about it. But you knew eventually I would have to go there!

And the reason I have to "go there" is because this story is nothing short of completely and utterly remarkable. It has so much to say to us as "modern Catholics" that I can't even think of where to start. If you haven't read the story lately, you will find it at Luke 24:13-35.

Of course the most exciting part of the story comes when Jesus breaks bread with the disciples and, in the midst of that Eucharistic event, their eyes are opened and they finally recognize him. It's a big moment. It's beautiful! But then...*he vanished from their sight!* Just at the moment when they finally *really saw him.* Just at the moment when his words about the Scriptures erupted into an experience of understanding. Just at the moment when they discover *he is risen!* Just at the moment when they *recognize Jesus Christ,* fully alive, human and divine, present on the road, present in the breaking of bread, present at their table – risen and present and close enough to reach out and touch! *Just at that moment,* he vanishes from their sight.

Friends, Jesus has vanished from my sight. So many times. More than I can count. I too have been on the road or in Scripture or at table or at Eucharist and caught a glimpse of the Lord, only to have him slip very quickly from the grasp of my mind and heart. I too have blinked and found him gone. Does the presence of the Risen Lord permeate my life? I pray that is so. But am I always intimately connected with him, close enough to reach out and touch? Do I live in a state of always seeing and recognizing him? No, I do not.

And I am not dismayed by this. In fact, as the years pass, I grow ever more content with this natural rhythm of the spiritual life. The disciples had beautiful moments with Jesus. They also had times of unknowing and distance, times of slowness of heart or blurred vision. This experience with the Risen Lord – he *vanished* from their sight – but they did not fret over it or desperately try to call him back or spend much time suffering over the loss. No, it seems they were quite filled by the experience, brief as it was. They ran with joy to tell the others. But of course you remember the story – their hearts were burning!

Lord, give me eyes to see you and a heart that burns long after you vanish from my sight!

A TEXAN'S TRIBUTE TO THE
LONG, HARD WINTER

Every winter, usually sometime toward the end of February, I begin to ask myself how in the world I ended up in the state of Connecticut. I meander through my mind and the chain of events that brought me here, and I always come to the same conclusion: this is where I belong. But it doesn't make winter any shorter.

As a native Texan, I doubt that the kind of winters I experience in the Northeast will ever be easy for me. In fact, I've noticed they aren't even easy for the people who have lived here all their lives. Just about every year they say, "That was a tough winter!" Even when tough is normal, it is still tough.

What I like most about winter is the way we all get through it together. It's rare to be out shoveling snow alone. There's always a neighbor or two out, suffering along with you. You always have something to discuss with strangers at the store. We ask each other, "Are we going to make it?" or we just call out across the street some quick word of commiseration as we dash to and from our cars (if you can "dash" across an icy driveway). I'll always remember a sweet moment after Mass one Sunday when I saw a priest lean down and encourage one of his elderly parishioners: "You'll only need that fleece for about one more week."

Another thing I like about winter is that it ends. When the warmth of spring hits, we all find our way outside – to the beach, to the park, or on a trail. Here we find camaraderie too. We got through it together. We did our time, we endured. We never really lost hope that there would indeed come a day when we could leave the fleece jacket at home. We feel we earned this beautiful day.

Perhaps it is simply my own determination to find some meaning in the personal challenge that winter poses for me, but I find winter to be a profound metaphor for the natural cycles of suffering that we endure in life and for the Paschal Mystery itself. Of course this isn't an original idea. But now that I've actually lived through what I can honestly call a *hard winter* – now I really get it.

I treasure three seasons in Connecticut, and I endure one. The beauty of the other three seasons is only enhanced by my memories of winter, by the ways winter has influenced and changed me. And in this I am reminded that the Risen Christ still bore – *still bears* – the wounds of crucifixion (Lk. 24:39; Jn. 20:25). The victorious Lamb worshiped in the Book of Revelation is *the Lamb who was slain* (Rev. 5).

And this is as it should be. Some wounds, forged in the toughest of times, should never be forgotten –

especially those which bring forth new life. No, we never forget about winter here in the Northeast. Winter is part of who we are. But we know and we believe that even the hardest winter leads to spring – always has, always will.

* * *

GOD'S NATIVE LANGUAGE

"Silence is God's first language."

St. John of the Cross

* * *

THE BARRENNESS OF BUSYNESS AND THE FRUITLESSNESS OF WORRY

If I asked a room full of Americans what plagues them most, I imagine that many would identify *busyness* and *worry* as major culprits. Demanding schedules and the stress of daily life are common contemporary burdens. At some point, we all fall victim to their debilitating effects.

I suppose these are not only contemporary burdens; they are timelessly human. Even thousands of years ago, Socrates wrote: "Beware the barrenness of a busy life." And another wise man – Jesus – taught: "Can any of you by worrying add a single moment to your life?" (Mt. 6:27).

Of course, sometimes it is good to be busy. We may be helping others, or working to make a living, or busily but happily fulfilling family responsibilities. But being busy becomes a barren enterprise when our schedules are so full that we lose ourselves, we forget about God, and we miss the whole point of life. We are totally disoriented but too busy to realize it! When this happens, our lives become barren because we are running in circles but getting nowhere. We are checking things off long lists, but deep inside ourselves, we are accomplishing nothing.

Like busyness, worry can have a valid role in our lives. Sometimes worrying motivates us to care for others or accomplish something. But worrying becomes fruitless when it paralyzes us, when it becomes all-consuming and prevents us from living, loving and growing. When this happens, we begin to sink deeper and deeper into fears and "what-ifs." We move farther and farther away from the simplicity of the love commands, the comfort of trusting God, and the serenity of the peaceful life we all long for.

It is hard, perhaps impossible, to simply tell ourselves to stop worrying and then do it. It is almost as hard to just stop being busy. But if we feel that worry and busyness are getting the upper hand in our lives, perhaps it is time to have a conversation with God. It is time to ask him: *"Am I too busy? Is my family too busy? What are we missing? How is my worry affecting others? How is it preventing me from being the person you want me to be? How are my busyness and worry preventing me from loving you and others?"*

If we take these questions to prayer with open minds and hearts, we may be surprised by how God asks us to change our lives and by the peace he wishes to give us. We may find ourselves reassessing our priorities and trusting God with our futures a bit more than we have in the past. We may remember that prayer, in and of itself, is a simple antidote to a hectic, anxious life.

Busyness leads to barrenness, and worry to waste. Instead, Jesus urges us toward a more deliberate, fruitful life. Let's talk to him about it.

"Therefore I tell you, do not worry about your life, what you will eat or what you will drink, or about your body, what you will wear. Is not life more than food, and the body more than clothing? Look at the birds of the air; they neither sow nor reap nor gather into barns, and yet your heavenly Father feeds them. Are you not of more value than they? And can any of you by worrying add a single hour to your span of life? And why do you worry about clothing? Consider the lilies of the field, how they grow; they neither toil nor spin, yet I tell you, even Solomon in all his glory was not clothed like one of these. But if God so clothes the grass of the field, which is alive today and tomorrow is thrown into the oven, will he not much more clothe you – you of little faith? Therefore do not worry, saying, 'What will we eat?' or 'What will we drink?' or 'What will we wear?' For it is the Gentiles who strive for all these things; and indeed your heavenly Father knows that you need all these things. But strive first for the kingdom of God and his righteousness, and all these things will be given to you as well. So do not worry about tomorrow, for tomorrow will bring worries of its own. Today's trouble is enough for today" (Mt. 6:25-34).

THE DEATH OF OUR LOVED ONES
MAKES OUR DEATHS EASIER

When I was in sixth grade, on a beautiful day in early September, my best friend's mother died. The date was September 8, the feast day of the Birth of Mary. My friend's mother was a faithful Catholic, and her name was Mary. I wanted to believe there was some connection. I wanted to believe that death had meaning and purpose. I wanted to believe that God had not abandoned this family.

This was my first real experience with death. Watching my friend process and accept her mother's death was an education. I saw the pain in her family, but there was an undercurrent of hope that made it all just bearable. Perhaps some measure of her mother's own faith remained in the hearts of each member of the family, and they wisely clung to it.

Hope in God does not stop death. It did not stop the death of Jesus. But it provides a fuller perspective on living and dying. It is the horizon that prevents us from becoming totally disoriented in an uncertain world. It is the invitation to believe that the end of a temporal life is but the beginning of an eternal one.

When my grandmother died some years later, I clung to that same Christian hope. I imagined her reuniting with all of her friends and family members who had passed on before her. And I imagined our own reunion in the future. I realized then that when my time came, my own death would be easier because I knew someone was waiting for me on the other side – a family member, someone close to me. I realized that even in death our loved ones serve us. Their deaths makes our own deaths easier. They have gone before us to share in the triumph of Christ and the power of his resurrection. With Christ, they say to us, "I go to prepare a place for you . . . so that where I am, there you may be also" (Jn. 14:3).

In the parish of my youth, tucked away in a side office, there was a cross on the wall. On the cross was a placid but triumphant Christ the King. Arms outstretched on what an old prayer called his "instrument of torture," his face, his raiment, his body seemed to say: *Take that, death! Look at me! I am healthy and robust! On this cross, I wear a crown! For everlasting!* It was an image of Christian hope, that orienting horizon.

The pain of death is part of life, and we share it with those we love. But our hope is in what comes next, in what we will share with them when our own time comes. Our hope is in the triumph of Christ, the God who raised him from the dead, and the place he has prepared for all of us to be together. If it were not so, Jesus said, I would have told you (Jn. 14:2).

ROMANCE

I recently heard a speaker quote Oswald Chambers:

"Get into the habit of saying, 'Speak, Lord,' and life will become a romance."

I was struck by the idea, and I tried putting it into practice. Changing a diaper, sitting in traffic, watching the news or working, I said, *"Speak, Lord."* It was a simple thing to do, a simple way to invite God in and allow him to speak to me when otherwise I would have just been listening to myself. I became more aware of his presence.

But what does Chambers mean by *"romance"*?

When we love someone, especially if we are *in love* with them, we want to be with them. We want to share everything with them. This is a natural and relatable human experience. As it turns out, we are *with God* all the time, but we rarely call out to him. We rarely seek the God who is hiding in plain sight in our world, in our day, in each moment. We are with the one we love, but we don't realize it. We aren't listening for the quiet voice of the beloved.

Jesus described this pervasive divine presence in his own way: "The Kingdom of God is among you" (Lk. 17:21). Indeed, the presence, the reign, the kingdom of

God grows, like a mustard seed, from something very small into a wonderful, shady bush where birds can land and rest (Lk. 13:18-19). It grows this way in our lives, too, as we become more aware of how close he is, how much he loves us and how much there is to share. The harsh world outside can feel more like a shady bush if we are living in it with the one we love.

Sounds romantic, doesn't it?

Speak, Lord!

* * *

WALK THE WALK

"Whoever says, 'I abide in him,'
ought to walk just as he walked."

1 John 2:6

* * *

LET THE SUN DO ITS WORK

Spring has finally come to Connecticut, which means a beautiful light through the trees and everyone gathering outside – fixing up the yard, starting a garden, or walking at the beach. Remember that sunny day I told you about? The one that finally comes, when you know you can leave the fleece behind for good? The one we earned with every miserably cold morning and every slip on the ice? That day has arrived!

It's that time of year when the sunblock comes out and reclaims its spot near the back door. But it usually takes a surprise or two before I take the sunblock seriously. On Sunday, after just an hour or two at the beach, my son's faces were a shade darker, and my own arms had lost the "winter white." The sun had done its work without me realizing what was happening.

The sun works on us with a silent, gradual, transforming power. If I go to the beach and stare at my skin, I don't see a change taking place. It's only later that evening when I look in the mirror that I see the change – the warm glow of color restored, the abiding result of happy times spent in warmth and light.

Below is a brief excerpt from Fr. Murray Bodo's *Landscape of Prayer*. Fr. Bodo shares a charming account of a fellow Franciscan who taught folks to pray before the Blessed Sacrament. He wanted them to stop trying so hard. He wanted them to stop stressing about "what to do." He wanted them to enjoy their time in this Eucharistic Presence in the same natural way that I enjoyed the warm sun at the beach with my kids. He wanted them to "let the sun do its work." And then later – as they went about their lives or glanced in the mirror – later they might discover that they had been changed.

"Brother Carlo used to expose the Blessed Sacrament in the monstrance and ask those who would learn to pray to sit in silence for two hours before the Blessed Sacrament. Usually they were, to say the least, nonplussed. And he would then explain, 'Imagine you are lying on the beach, thinking of nothing in particular, just letting the sun's rays work gradually on your skin, a beautiful tan emerging day by day. The host in the monstrance is the sun. Just be in its presence, not worrying about so-called distractions or whether or not you are concentrating on the 'sun.' A change gradually takes place in you the way a suntan emerges on the skin. Relax, let the 'sun' do its work. Your work is to be there'" (Fr. Murray Bodo, OFM, Landscape of Prayer, St. Anthony Messenger Press).

* * *

A VERSE WORTH MEMORIZING

Each year my Catholic Biblical School classes spend seven weeks reading and wrestling with ten of St. Paul's letters. Reading St. Paul plunges us into something that is simultaneously transcendent and down-to-earth, mystical and practical, inspiring and instructive. This tension – which Paul maintains with every stroke of the pen – deftly delivers something that modern readers find elusive in their own lives: the integration of "real life" and "the spiritual life." Remember, Paul was first and foremost a missionary, secondly a pastor (a *shepherd*), and only thirdly a theologian. What Paul wrote, he wrote for a purpose – for real people facing real problems, for Christian communities struggling just like our communities do today. His theology emerged from "real life."

The Second Letter to the Corinthians is one of my favorite Pauline books. In it we witness Paul's passion for the Gospel, his love for his people, his zeal, his temper, his sense of humor and his creativity. The book also provides rich examples of Paul's theology presented in the context of "real life" situations. One such example is found in 2 Cor. 1:15-24. Here Paul is offering a bit of self-defense. The Corinthian community was apparently miffed with him because he did not visit them as he had planned. They accused him of vacillating, of being unreliable. Paul heard about this and wanted to address it. He wanted to assure them that he changed his mind for a reason, not simply on a whim or because he cared little for the community.

In this situation, most of us would simply write, "I did not come because (insert your excuse here)." But it's almost as though Paul can't stop thinking about, writing about, teaching about Jesus Christ! For him, Christ is the foundation of all things, the answer to all things. And so his explanation of why he did not visit Corinth becomes yet another opportunity to teach about the goodness of God in Christ Jesus:

> *"Was I vacillating when I wanted to do this? Do I make my plans according to ordinary human standards, ready to say 'Yes, yes' and 'No, no' at the same time? As surely as God is faithful, our word to you has not been 'Yes and No.' For the Son of God, Jesus Christ, whom we proclaimed among you...was not 'Yes and No'; but in him it is always 'Yes.' For in him every one of God's promises is a 'Yes.' For this reason it is through him that we say the 'Amen', to the glory of God" (2 Cor. 1:17-20).*

We can see how Paul's self-defense quickly flows into an account of God's own faithfulness. Paul does not vacillate weakly between "yes" and "no" – for he is a follower of Jesus Christ, who does not vacillate; he believes in a God who keeps every promise!

One verse from this section really struck me as I studied it this year. It's just like St. Paul to put all the pieces together with a statement like this:

> *"In him [Jesus Christ] every one of God's promises is a 'Yes.'"*

Would it be going too far to say that this verse sums up all of Scripture? It is surely a verse worth memorizing, a verse worth imprinting on our hearts.

May we always take comfort in the faithfulness of our God, remembering that in Jesus Christ, every one of God's promises – to his people, to his Church, to our families, to each one of us – is an emphatic "Yes!" And following Paul's example, let us remember how deep we can go, and how profound our knowledge of Christ can be, even in the midst of real life.

* * *

I BELIEVE IN DINOSAURS

Indulge me for a moment in a strange memory. I was standing in the Museum of Natural History in Washington, D.C., in the dinosaur exhibit, in front of one of those huge reconstructed dinosaur skeletons (a brontosaurus, I think). I looked at it for a while, not really thinking much about it one way or another. Then I glanced down and noticed a replica of a little baby dinosaur, curled up at the big dinosaur's feet. It was very small and sleeping, and it was very close to where I was standing. Something about the replica held my gaze and for several long moments – I was totally transfixed, totally focused on the baby brontosaurus.

Suddenly I had a strange and profound realization: *Dinosaurs actually existed!*

But I knew that already! *Didn't I?*

I don't know what amazed me more – my newfound belief in dinosaurs or the discovery that *I had apparently not really believed in dinosaurs for my whole life!* Like everyone else, I had learned about dinosaurs since childhood. I never got especially excited about them, but I certainly had no reason to doubt their existence. And yet in that moment at the museum, I realized that I had never really allowed myself to believe – to imagine, to grasp, to fall into – a reality where these fantastic creatures actually lived and breathed and mated and ate each other, long before human beings existed – in *my world* – in *Texas* for goodness sake! Looking at that baby dino, I suddenly "got it." The truth broke in, and I imagined and believed in a world of dinosaurs, a time before humans, something incredible but true.

This experience in the museum happened to me as an adult. When I realized that I hadn't actually believed in dinosaurs even though I thought I did, I wondered about all the other things I think I believe. I wondered about God and Jesus, forgiveness and Eucharist. I wondered about heaven and hell, death and forever. I wondered about the little doubts that nag at me sometimes and the big things I take for granted. I realized there are things I never really let myself imagine and things I want to imagine but can't.

It seems that part of being human is not fully knowing our own minds. I *thought* I believed in dinosaurs, but in reality, I was only *coming to believe* in them. And so it is with the truths of our faith. Do we believe in them? Yes, we do. And we don't. And we might. And we will.

For now, we can add to our daily prayer the honest words of the father of a convulsing boy, who pleaded with Jesus: "I believe! Help my unbelief!" (Mk. 9:24)

DO WE REALLY WANT HEAVEN?

Have you ever secretly thought that heaven sounds boring? Let's face it, for beings who live in time, an eternity of peace and joy can actually sound unpleasantly monotonous! What will it really be like? Won't we grow tired of eating the banquet, beholding the vision, and coasting along in a state of bliss?

In C.S. Lewis' wonderful little book, *The Problem of Pain*, he gives a simple response to those who say they aren't sure they want heaven. Heaven is not a mind-numbing forever of boring, sweet goodness. Heaven, he explains, is the "other piece," that thing you have been yearning for but couldn't put into words, that memory you keep going back to, the reality you've only peeked at in fleeting moments. It's the thing you love most in every book you've read, the satisfaction you have in your work, the understanding you share with a friend, the "secret signature of each soul."

The satisfaction of these things is not a static or monotonous reality. It is not a one-time experience that quickly grows old. There is dynamism here, relationship, giving over, connection, a unity in diversity that you only glimpsed before. Heaven is something you already knew but rediscover forever.

Here is an excerpt from C.S. Lewis' *The Problem of Pain:*

"There have been times when I think we do not desire heaven; but more often I find myself wondering whether, in our heart of hearts, we have ever desired anything else. You may have noticed that the books you really love are bound together by a secret thread. You know very well what is the common quality that makes you love them, though you cannot put it into words: but most of your friends do not see it at all.... Even in your hobbies, has there not always been some secret attraction which the others are curiously ignorant of – something, not to be identified with, but always on the verge of breaking through, the smell of cut wood in the workshop or the clap-clap of water against the boat's side? Are not all lifelong friendships born at the moment when at last you meet another human being who has some inkling (but faint and uncertain even in the best) of that something which you were born desiring, and which, beneath the flux of other desires and in all the momentary silences between the louder passions, night and day, year by year, from childhood to old age, you are looking for, watching for, listening for? You have never had it. All the things that have ever deeply possessed your soul have been but hints of it – tantalizing glimpses, promises never quite fulfilled, echoes that died away just as they caught your ear. But if it should really become manifest – if there ever came an echo that did not die away but swelled into the sound itself – you would know it. Beyond all possibility of doubt you would say 'Here at last is the thing I was made for.'

We cannot tell each other about it. It is the secret signature of each soul, the incommunicable and unappeasable want, the thing we desired before we met our wives or made our friends or chose our work, and which we shall still desire on our deathbeds, when the mind no longer knows wife or friend or work. While we are, this is. If we lose this, we lose all."

* * *

ENOUGH SAID

"Perfect love casts out fear."

1 John 4:18

* * *

OUR FOREST IS BURNING

For the past year or so, I have enjoyed a creative correspondence with a gifted poet named Scott Eagan. I was delighted to discover that Scott lives and farms at Madonna House, the ongoing apostolate of one of my favorite spiritual guides, Servant of God Catherine Doherty. Within the Madonna House community, Scott lives the simplicity and quiet of the Holy Family of Nazareth. He works the land, he prays and writes.

Scott's poems reveal the heart of a farmer, one who is close to the land. In a time when so many of us are to a certain extent disconnected from nature, Scott's poems provide an intimate window into the beauty of rural Canada, the changing seasons, farm animals, wild animals, harvests and crops, sun, moon and stars. My own world is broadened by the images he shares and his interpretations of life and nature.

I'm thankful to Scott for allowing me to share some of his work on my blog and in this book.

This particular poem was inspired by the Canadian wildfires of 2016. As I'm sure you will agree, it also resonates with the fires that rage within.

Dry Lightning

The air is charged
overfull with heat and smoke and ash
our forest is burning
beast of a wildfire bearing down
torching the houses, the place where we live
we can only pray for rain.

Try as we may, no tears
it is all consuming, nothing left unscorched
flashes from heaven to earth
and from earth to heaven explode as they meet
thunder rolls round the heart
we watch, we wait, we run
while the flames rage in their course
and inside us, the rains pour.

* * *

©2016 Scott Eagan

ALL IS VANITY!

There are a few books of the Bible that I really find amusing. My students know that one of them is the Book of Tobit. In fact I apparently made one too many jokes about the book and was pointedly told by one of my students (thank you, Sr. Mahilia) that I needed to rein it in!

The Book of Ecclesiastes is another book that amuses me. That is, when it isn't making me totally depressed! Let's put it this way – Ecclesiastes may not be the book to read when you're already having a bad day.

The best-known verse in the Book of Ecclesiastes is probably: "Vanity of vanities! All is vanity" (1:2). "Vanity" is the typical English translation of the Hebrew word *hebel*, which literally means *vapor* or *breath*. The word is used 38 times in the Book of Ecclesiastes to describe the fleeting and even futile nature of life. The Good News Bible (not known for its technical accuracy, but pretty good at capturing the "gist" of things) even goes so far as to translate the verse this way: "It is useless, useless. Life is useless, all useless."

The author goes on to write other things we might find surprising. Seeking wisdom, he says, is an "unhappy business" (1:13); there is nothing better for human beings than to eat and drink (2:24); we aren't really any better off than animals, not in life or death (3:18-21); and the dead (all of them) "know nothing" and "have no reward" (9:5).

Sure, there are a few uplifting verses in Ecclesiastes (a lovely passage on the value of friendship, for example; 4:9-12), and the author does retain and encourage a stalwart faith in the midst of his observations of life's futilities (3:12-14; 4:18-20). But those who try to paint over this book with an overly optimistic gloss are ignoring its brooding tone and many of its grim messages.

Some have even questioned whether this unusual book belongs in the canon of Scripture. After all, doesn't the maxim "life is vanity" contradict the basic biblical belief that life is a sacred gift from God? But there is a stark realism here, written down and poured out on the sacred page. That is why I don't find it strange that the Book of Ecclesiastes found its way into the canon. I don't think the ideas we read here mean that life really is *hebel*, or futile. I don't think the author's own uncertainty about the after-life means that we need to be uncertain. But this book allows us to express our frustrations and fears, and it comforts us. It allows us to have dark moments and say, "I don't get it" and "It isn't fair." It allows us to read and say "I'm not sure either" and "What is death, really?"

If nothing else, this special book reminds us that opening the Bible always begins a conversation with God. We can express every emotion, ask every question, and enter into every mystery. And when we enter into the very honest and very human ideas we find in the Book of Ecclesiastes, we can be assured that our God understands and responds: "I hear you, my people. Keep talking to me."

* * *

TO CHANGE THE WORLD

"An authentic faith –
which is never comfortable
or completely personal – always involves
a deep desire to change the world."

Pope Francis, Evangelii Gaudium 183

* * *

HOMILY GEM #2

Heard on Sunday: *"When praying for someone who is sick, you can use the words of Lazarus' sisters, who said to Jesus: Lord, the one you love is ill."* Fr. Declan was referring to the story of the raising of Lazarus (John 11:1-44).

How did Jesus respond to Mary and Martha when they sent word that their brother was ill? He said, "This illness is not to end in death." Of course, several verses later, we find out that Lazarus has indeed died. And yet with Mary and Martha, we know this is not the end. We believe the words of Jesus, "Your brother will rise."

Do you have a loved one or a friend who is facing a serious illness? This story from John's Gospel is fertile ground for prayer and reflection: the delay of Jesus in coming to Lazarus' side, the faith of the sisters, the tears of Jesus, the power of his voice that raised Lazarus from the tomb, the unbinding of death's trappings, the foreshadowing of Jesus' own death and triumph.

Lord, the one you love is ill. I trust you. You know what is best. In your time, raise him, untie him and let him go free.

* * *

THE REST OF MY LIFE,
THE BEST OF MY LIFE

I recently took my daughter to a music lesson with her new saxophone teacher. We went downstairs into his music studio, and I sat down at a table to work while they continued on into the next room for the lesson. I fully intended to be productive for the next half hour.

It wasn't so much the sound of horns and laughter coming from the next room that distracted me (I'm used to that!). It was the collection of newspaper clippings, inspirational messages, jokes and pictures of Snoopy that hung all around the walls of the studio. Everywhere I looked, something interesting caught my eye. After I had read and enjoyed some of them, I got out my work and tried to focus. But one more message was propped up on the table, printed on a block of wood. It said: *I'm going to make THE REST of my life THE BEST of my life.*

Now some of you older folks will laugh at me or protest, but let me say it . . . I will soon be entering (if I haven't already!) the *second half* of my life. And I don't care if you're pushing 40, 70 or 95 – at some point in your life, a little voice in your head begins to whisper the words: *My best years are behind me.*

I don't think there's anything wrong with looking at the past with joy and nostalgia. There's nothing wrong with recognizing the beauty of youth or yearning a bit for the days when we had more energy and a higher metabolism. But no matter how wistful we may be for the good things of the past, the future will always lie ahead of us as gift. The future is unknown, and with this comes great possibility – the possibility that the best may actually be yet to come.

But the best years won't come by chance. As we get older, it is easy to just settle in and "be ourselves" and "do what we always do." It is easy to maintain the status quo. But the life we really want to lead before our God and before each other requires so much more than that.

Our future lies ahead as a merging of God's grace and our own free will, a melding of God's plans and our own, a partnership between human and divine that can lead to amazing things. Maybe God wants us to accomplish something great. Maybe he wants us to give some profound service. Or maybe he just wants us to be totally devoted to someone who needs us.

You know the bumper sticker: *God isn't finished with me yet.* Well, he isn't. And that's kind of exciting. The future lies ahead as gift. I'm going to make the rest of my life the best of my life.

* * *

FRIENDS WITH GOD?

In a weekly blog post, I asked my readers:

Can we be friends with God?

It's easy to quickly answer "yes" to this question. I'm thinking of those great bumper stickers that say "My best friend is a carpenter." But I asked readers to carefully consider the nature of friendship: *How would you define friendship? Reflecting on this definition, would you consider God to be your friend? Or is your relationship with God something else entirely?*

I received some wonderful and candid responses on the blog, by email and on Facebook. I learned so much from and about the folks who sent me their thoughts. One of my readers, Jim, sent me a thoughtful list of questions that reflect on the nature of friendship and what it might mean to be friends with God. I'd like to share Jim's response with you here:

Being a friend of God is an awesome question. I think about what that personally means to me and ask myself what it means to be a friend and does this apply to being God's friend:

Do I stay in touch on a regular basis?

Do I put my trust in him?

Would I let him take any of my treasured possessions?

Would I rely on my friend to do the same for me as I would do for him?

Would I intentionally do anything to harm him in any way?

Would I drop everything and go with him if he needed me?

Would I defend his name if he was falsely accused of something?

Would I tell others about him and what he means to me?

Would I easily introduce him to others and not worry about their reactions?

Would I always believe in him?

Would I never abandon him?

Would I give my life for him?

* * *

FRIENDS WITH GOD? DREAM ON.

The overwhelming response to my question about whether or not we can be friends with God was yes – emphatically, yes! Some readers were clear that they *know* God can be their friend because *he already is*! Others added helpful distinctions. God is a different kind of friend than our buddies or even our human soulmates.

I agree. If the question were simply asked on a philosophical level, I might wonder. I might surmise that it was wishful thinking on the part of human beings to aspire to be "friends" with God. But as usual, Scripture sets me straight, and that's just the way I like it. Vatican II refers to Scripture as "the words of God expressed in human language" (*Dei Verbum* 13). I can't think of a better way to learn about friendship with God.

The first Scripture verse that always comes to mind when I think about being God's friend is Exodus 33:11: "Thus the Lord used to speak to Moses face to face, *as one speaks to a friend*." The transcendent God of the Israelites was talking with Moses? No matter how awesome Moses was (and he was), he was still a human being, a creature, an imperfect person. But there was an intimacy between God and Moses that went down in Israelite lore as genuine friendship.

Abraham was another ancient who was called God's friend. He is described as such three times in the Bible: 2 Chronicles 20:7, Isaiah 41:8, and James 2:23. How would you like it if this is how people described you? What if, instead of "short lady with curly brown hair and a bunch of kids," people said of me, "You know, Amy, the friend of God?" Gulp! God give me the faith of Abraham!

Jesus, of course, called his disciples his friends. And not only his disciples. Remember this one: "The Son of Man came eating and drinking, and they say, 'Look, a glutton and a drunkard, a friend of tax collectors and sinners!'" (Matt. 11:19)? This was an *accusation* levelled at Jesus – *friend of sinners!* Never has a truer accusation been made!

Of course, we would be entirely remiss on the topic if we did not recall the remarkable words of Jesus, said in farewell to his eleven faithful disciples (Judas had left the table): "This is my commandment, that you love one another as I have loved you. No one has greater love than this, to lay down one's life for one's friends. You are my friends if you do what I command you. I do not call you servants any longer, because the servant does not know what the master is doing; but I have called you friends, because I have made known to you everything that I have heard from my Father. You did not choose me but I chose you" (Jn. 15:12-16). No commentary needed. These are words to pray by.

And finally, I share with you a passage that says it all. Yes, Judas had left the table, only to be reunited with Jesus in the garden, where he would kiss Jesus and betray him unto death, even death on a cross. How did Jesus address Judas as he approached him in the garden? Yes, he called him "friend" (Mt. 26:50).

Catherine Doherty wrote that "all men who have religion of some sort are dreamers, and dreamers of a very special kind. They dream of unity between God and men."

Friendship is about intimacy. It is an intentional intimacy. One reader aptly quoted the wisdom of St. Catherine of Siena: "God is closer to us than water is to a fish." This is the stuff of dreamers, indeed. But we know this dream is true. So dream on, friends of God, dream on!

* * *

ADVENT & CHRISTMAS

THEN TIME IS ALWAYS OURS

As the longest, darkest days of winter approach, and as we wait with both patience and impatience for the birth of our Savior, I would like to share with you another poem by Scott Eagan.

If we learn to appreciate the gift of each season, the rhythm of life that God has prescribed, then no time is ever fallow, no season is ever wasted.

And so before we look forward to spring, may we pay winter our respects, and find in her darkest night the Gift that, like nature herself, can never be rushed – the long-awaited unity between God and human beings.

Winter Time

Times change
what once was our summer
warm sun and rains
almost as if God had smiled on
every solid working day
and every blessed night of rest...
then autumn passed
crimson and gold washed away
by cold, grey rains
through gusty winds of passage
and we are left with winter.

Our axis has tilted
our face turned north of the sun
almost as if His face has frowned
warm rains become white flakes
cold on the cheek, melting
on our summer passed by
washing across our autumn
now clinging to winter time.

Know that if we wait
if we may learn to enjoy frost
the cold and the crystal
the days when our face, low
to the sun's waning light
– yet a loving face nonetheless –
perceiving the distant possibility of spring
and its rising warm smile to return
then time is always ours.

* * *

© 2015 Scott Eagan

WHY WE STILL NEED JOHN THE BAPTIST

During Advent, we always encounter John the Baptist in the Sunday Gospel readings. John is a colorful figure, and we all love him for it. But we might not love him so much if we met him in the desert! Especially if he was shouting in our direction!

There's a wonderful question in Luke's account of the birth of John the Baptist. When John was born, people asked themselves: "What then will this child become?" (Lk. 1:66).

What *did* John become? And why is he still so important?

Luke's Gospel identifies John as the prophet who came to smooth rough ways by levelling mountains and filling in valleys. That sounds like hard work. And it is. Because when it comes to the human heart, most of us have no interest in having our mountains levelled or our valleys filled in. We go through our days saying, "I'm just fine, thank you," continuing right along the same rough path as always. It was John's momentous task to convince people that they are not fine. As Jesus would later explain, "Those who are healthy do not need a physician, but the sick do" (Lk. 5:31). It is hard work convincing people that they need a physician. How often have you put off a visit to the doctor? How often have you ignored pains and symptoms, hoping they would go away on their own? John's preaching convinced people that they could no longer ignore the symptoms. And so they repented, making way for a healing Savior.

John was a sight to see, a man of the desert, and I imagine his prophetic voice was quite loud. We still need that loud voice ringing in our ears, that strange sight of someone so different telling us that something is not right in our lives, in our world. Our own spiritual blindness, our self-satisfied complacency, is the impenetrable fortress John wanted to knock down.

This was the work of the one who was not even worthy to loosen the strap of Jesus' sandal! This was the preparation for something even greater. So imagine – *imagine* – what *Jesus* can do in our hearts if first we listen to the voice of the Baptist!

* * *

HOW NICHOLAS *REALLY* BECAME SANTA

In an effort to keep my five-year-old son informed about who Santa Claus really is, I asked him to watch a video my daughters enjoyed when they were his age entitled *Nicholas: The Boy Who Became Santa.* Of course, this was his last choice behind *Ninjago, Miles from Tomorrowland,* and *Peppa Pig.* But he did watch the video. When he wandered into the kitchen after it ended, I asked him, "So how did Nicholas become Santa?" With a little shrug, Julian said, "He grew a beard."

One might say that Julian had missed the entire point. Or perhaps he summed it all up with a keen observation. To grow a beard is to grow up. Nicholas grew up. He grew a beard. He grew older. It turned white. And indeed, somewhere in this living, growing, and aging process, he became "Santa" – holy, a saint.

So how did Nicholas become Santa? He grew up. Too simplistic? Maybe.

Whether you grow a beard this year, or maybe just a few new wrinkles, I'm sure you will all grow wiser and hopefully a little more "santa." I'm happy to be journeying and growing and, yes, aging with all of you. Happy, joyous, prosperous and transformative New Year, friends!

* * *

THE RIGHT GIFT FOR A SAVIOR

The iconic image of wise men breaking open their treasure chests before the child Jesus is a powerful one (Mt. 2:11). The magi travelled a great distance to bring gifts of wealth and luxury, gifts fit for a king. This is how they paid him homage.

The beautiful story of the magi may lead us to ask what gifts we will bring Jesus. What does he want from us?

To understand what Jesus wants, we must first ask why he has come into our hearts and into our world. The Gospels answer clearly: "He will save his people" (Mt. 1:21). This is not just a King but a Savior! Can the gifts we bring acknowledge this even more magnificent mission?

Yes. They can and they should. We must bring him the things a Savior wants most – *the things within us that need saving.* We need not travel from east to west but only deep within our own hearts, to bring out the things that lie hidden. These are the gifts Jesus wants. This is how we worship a Savior.

Lord Jesus, I lay before you the gold of my sins and weaknesses, the incense of my painful memories and relationships, and the myrrh of my fears and anxieties.

These do not seem like gifts fit for a King, and yet I know they are gifts worthy of a Savior. I offer them to you from the treasure-chest of my heart, knowing that you can transform and redeem them. I come to you open, empty and vulnerable; be a quiet, loving, saving presence in me. Amen.

* * *

LENT & EASTER

A 12-YEAR-OLD'S STATIONS OF THE CROSS

I am so happy to share with you something that my daughter wrote and shared with me. It is hard to describe how I felt when I read these Stations of the Cross. Siobhan, I'm so proud to be your mom.

I. CONDEMNED - JUDGE

Stand before the crowd for me
What have you to say for thee?
No sound, no word to save his name
To end his pain, to stop his fate
Although his heart is pure and clean
He is condemned to endless sleep

II. CARRY - SPECTATOR

I watch them weave a crown of thorns
Hustle, heckle taunt and scorn
I watch them load your back with weight
Bitterness crossed with twisted hate
I want to end their cruel advance
But I do not move when I have the chance

III. FALLING - SOLDIER

You stumble yet we push you down
You cry but we ignore the sound
No one helps you when you fall
No one makes a move at all
I cannot help but feel for you
But when you're down I do not move

IV. MEETING - MOTHER

So alone you stumble forth
They do not know what you are worth
So now, now when you say to me
"Courage, woman, for this must be"
I truly know that I must believe
For by your cross we are redeemed

V. HELP - SIMON

They push and pull me toward the tree
The heavy burden meant for thee
They grow impatient tired of
Your slow progress or lack thereof
They snatch me off the streets of ill
So I help you against my will

VI. FACE - VERONICA

Alone again he struggles on
They will nail him to the tree anon
I don't have anything to give
But I cannot yet leave him
My hands I have and my veil in place
So at least I can wash your face

VII. FALLING AGAIN - PETER

I see you fall this time on rock
I cannot bare to see them mock
I have denied you thrice today
But still I love you, still I pray
That you'll forgive me for I was weak
As you set on humble and meek

VIII. CRY - WOMAN

As he stumbles toward us still
He is not drained of his good will
Though it's I who should help thee
You reach out and comfort me
You've been abandoned by your friends
But still you love until the end

IX. FALLING STILL - PHARISEE

This time he falls and does not rise
He is so close to his demise
That I can see the wasted land
Where they will nail his feet and hands
In spite of cards that fate has dealt
Why do you not save yourself?

X. ROBBED - JOHN

They take your clothes and leave you bare
Crown of thorns still in your hair
You wear those twigs like the king you are
And despite these horrid scars
I know you'll come again someday
So that we can then be saved

XI. NAILED - MAN

This is my job and I've no choice
But I have yet to hear your voice
You do not protest when we stab
Your hands and then your side they jab
I cannot help but think and pray
Are you the king as they all say?

XII. MORTEM - CHRIST

Father father why have you
Abandoned me as I go through
I trust you, I do not doubt
The things you ask to carry out
With my last breath, I want all to hear it:
Into your hands I commend my spirit

XIII. TAKEN - APOSTLE

His body hangs limp on the tree
Broken skin bleeding for me
They take him down with faith and tears
As the space around them clears
Though we left you on that cross
You promised to come back for us

XIV. BURIED - FATHER

They lay your body in the tomb
My spirit fills up the ashen room
You did not let this cup pass by
And still the world does not know why
Nails were driven through your skin
To save your beloved from their sins

GIVE IT UP

This year as we kick off our forty day fast, let's remember the "gift of limits." We have a chance to do something special here, something we may not be able to commit to or sustain for years, but that we *can* commit to for forty days.

I know giving up something like sweets, alcohol, snacks or television is no longer in vogue. But there is a reason "giving up" has been part of our tradition for so long. While no one thinks that giving up chocolate is more important than giving up gossip, making some kind of physical sacrifice helps both our minds and our bodies be aware that this is a special time devoted to something (Someone) much greater than our physical or entertainment desires. Every time we think of that thing that we want and then make that small sacrifice, we acknowledge the goodness of that thing but recognize the greater goodness of God. It's old-fashioned, yeah, I know, but it works like a charm! It is also a concrete way we tell God, "I'm willing to give up something for you, like you gave up something for me." When you think about it that way, giving up sweets or lattes seems remarkably easy.

If there is something you want to do such as give up gossip or visit the sick or attend an extra Mass per week, then by all means do those good things. We should all adopt such a spiritual practice, which offers a true fast, so very pleasing to God (Isa. 58:6-7). But find some small material sacrifice as well, something that keeps reminding you – body and soul – that you are setting your mind and heart on something even higher than the very good things of this wonderful world.

As a child once told me, "We give something up because he gave up everything for us."

* * *

STAY WITH ME

As Holy Week approaches, it may be useful to focus on one Gospel verse that can serve as your guide throughout these holiest of days. This time of year, there is so much going on personally and spiritually – having a theme or focus may help you "get it together" so you can walk with both serenity and purpose alongside Christ as he enters Jerusalem and embraces his fate on your behalf.

You may already have a favorite verse that can give you focus during these last weeks of Lent. Write it on a card or sticky note and place it somewhere you will see it at least a few times a day – near your computer or in your prayer book. Passages such as John 14-16, Philippians 2 or even Isaiah 53 offer a treasure-trove of possibilities.

Another favorite of mine, and one I offer you here, is found within the very poignant depiction of Jesus' last meal with his disciples as found in Luke's Gospel (Lk. 22:14-38). Here we witness an intimate scene between Jesus and his closest companions. The disciples – who have failed Jesus in the past and will fail him again in the very near future – are the objects of Jesus' love and affection. Jesus tells them how eagerly he has desired to share this meal with them (22:15), how his blood is poured out for them (22:20), and, even when they begin to argue over which of them is the greatest (note that this conversation takes place *immediately* after receiving the bread and wine given and poured out for them!), even when they again show this human frailty, Jesus patiently points them back toward humility (22:27) and then promises them the future bounty of his Kingdom (22:30). One might see in this passage – punctuated by the betrayal of Judas and the impending denials of Peter – a portrait of Jesus' undying love for sinners.

In the midst of this communion, Jesus says to his disciples: "You have stayed with me through all my trials" (22:28). It is bittersweet to know that these friends of Jesus will soon abandon him – first by sleeping and then by fleeing, leaving Jesus alone to face the brutality of his captors and a lonely death. But we cannot judge them. We also sleep and flee; we have also left him alone.

For these next few weeks, we can meditate on these gentle words of Jesus and the trusting expectation they hold: *"You have stayed with me through all my trials."* We often talk of trusting Jesus – but it seems *he also trusts us* – to stay with him, to be faithful, not to scatter. Perhaps our hearts must change if we wish to never betray this enormous, divine trust. But isn't that what Lent is all about?

Lord Jesus Christ, give me the strength and serenity, the focus and purpose, to stay with you. You believe in me and my love for you. I do not want to fail you. I do not want to sleep through this time. I do not want to abandon you for the cares of the world. Change my heart so I may love you more than I love myself. Change my heart so I do not turn away from your Cross. Change my heart so I may stay with you through all your trials.

* * *

PASCHAL MYSTERIES

"There have been times when,
after long on my knees in a cold chancel,
a stone has rolled from my mind,
and I have looked in and seen the old questions
lie folded and in a place by themselves,
like the piled grave clothes of love's risen body."

R.S. Thomas

* * *

ONE HOUR RETREAT FOR HOLY WEEK

Last year as Holy Week approached, I recommended reading all of Mark's Gospel in one sitting as a one-hour retreat experience. If you have not had a chance to do so, you may wish to try it this year. Try to forget everything you think you know about Jesus, sit in a quiet place, and listen to him. You will encounter a raw, passionate preacher and miracle-worker, one who has an urgent message for you.

If you have already read Mark, this year I recommend reading Jesus' Farewell Discourse in John's Gospel (John 14-16). These powerful and intimate words of Jesus are spoken at the Last Supper, after Jesus has washed the feet of his disciples and before he is betrayed in the garden. In his farewell address, Jesus offers words of comfort to his disciples. He reminds them of his unity with the Father and their unity with him. He urges them to love one another before he lays down his life for them.

You have read or heard these words before. They are beautiful, haunting, mystical, profound and personal. Are you a disciple of Jesus? Then he is speaking to you.

After class this past week, one of my students commented that John 14-16 should be required reading for every Christian, every few months. Indeed, we need this personal and profound reminder from Jesus, that if we do not love one another as he has loved us, if we do not lay down our lives for one another in small ways and large, then Jesus will not be present in this world. With the privilege of being Jesus' friend (15:15) comes the joyful and difficult responsibility of sharing that friendship with others (15:13). This is when he truly abides in us, and we in him (15:10).

Reflection Questions for John 14-16

What kinds of things would you say to your loved ones if you knew you were dying?

How do you think the disciples felt when Jesus told them he was leaving, and how does Jesus comfort them?

What is the relationship between Jesus and the Father, and what is their relationship with believers?

How will the Holy Spirit work in our lives in Jesus' absence?

What is the new commandment of Jesus? How does Jesus love? How must we love?

What does Jesus say that especially strikes you as you prayerfully read this text? What is he speaking to your heart? How do you respond to him?

GOOD FRIDAY: WE MUST DO THIS TOO

The word "disciple" means "learner." But what makes a disciple different from a student? A disciple is completely devoted to the teacher. A disciple walks along with the teacher, listening and changing because of him. A disciple might say something like, "I want to think like my teacher. I want to *be like* my teacher." A student departs at the end of the course. But a disciple remains at the feet of the teacher.

We are not students of Jesus Christ. We are disciples. As we follow him today along the Way of Salvation, we should also say, "I want to think like my teacher. I want to *be like* my teacher." Our teacher will not say much more to us. But he will act, and we will watch. We will see the greatest love of all, the kind that lays down its life for a friend. And so as disciples, we will see what we too must do.

One thing that makes this day so holy and so good is not only what he did, but what he teaches us to do. As is expected of disciples, we must continue the work of our teacher:

"We know love by this, that he laid down his life for us – and we ought to lay down our lives for one another" (1 Jn. 3:16).

* * *

BURYING THE ALLELUIA

As many of you know, I started my first parish job at the ripe old age of 23, and I had absolutely no idea what I was doing. Fortunately, my predecessor, Sister Blanche Twigg, had run a tight ship. It was just my job to keep it floating.

Sister Blanche had many gifts that I did not have, and one of these gifts was that she really knew how to work with children. She understood that they are both literal and mystical. I discovered this about Sister Blanche as my first Lent in the parish approached.

About a week before Ash Wednesday, my co-worker Cheryl (yes, the one who had oriented me around the large paint can in Waldorf) disappeared into the storage room, rummaged around for a bit, and emerged with an old banner that read "A-L-L-E-L-U-I-A!" She then informed me that it was almost time to bury it.

Apparently every year Sister Blanche would gather the children together and talk to them about Lent. Then she would fold up the big banner and symbolically bury it. "ALLELUIA" went dark until Easter, when it was once again allowed to see the light of day.

When I heard about this annual custom, I couldn't decide if it was a stroke of pedagogical genius or a hopelessly depressing gesture. Saying good-bye to

"ALLELUIA" was deeply symbolic but also really sad!

I thought about Sister Blanche's banner as I sat in church on Easter Sunday. A visiting priest, whose own father is dying in Africa, dug deep and gave of himself and filled the church with Easter laughter. Interwoven throughout genuine messages of faith, hope and love was humor that brought the room to life and charged it with Christian joy.

Easter laughter is a long, and some might say strange, tradition of the Church. There was a time when the liturgy actually called for a good joke during the Easter homily! Laughter expresses joy, even our joy that He is Risen. Even in church, even at Mass! Laughter connects us with others who share our joy and expresses the end of our waiting, the consummation of our longing, the last of our days without alleluias.

Friends, we have dug up the "ALLELUIA." He is risen, indeed!

* * *

PRAYERS

TRANSFIGURE ME, LORD:
AN AGING PRAYER

Saint Paul wrote, "We are not discouraged; rather, although our outer self is wasting away, our inner self is being renewed day by day" (2 Cor. 4:16). We are transfigured as we age, changed in outward appearance. But that change can correspond with a profound inner transformation, an inner illumination. Like the Transfigured Christ who changed outwardly, inside we can shine like the sun! And so as the years pass, we pray for that profound change, for the inner luminosity of wisdom, kindness, generosity, forgiveness and love.

* * *

Lord Jesus Christ, you were transfigured on a high mountain. In the sight of your friends, you began to shine like the sun. Transfigure me too, inside and out, that your light may shine in and through me – into your world, among your people, and all the way into your heavenly presence.

As each year passes, *transfigure me, Lord.*
As I see myself changing, *transfigure me, Lord.*
When I am no longer young, *transfigure me, Lord.*
As my body slows down, *transfigure me, Lord.*
In my aches and pains, *transfigure me, Lord.*
When I face illness, *transfigure me, Lord.*

When I cannot work, *transfigure me, Lord.*
When I lose my parents, *transfigure me, Lord.*
If I lose my spouse, *transfigure me, Lord.*
When I lose my friends, *transfigure me, Lord.*
When my life seems stagnant, *transfigure me, Lord.*
When I do not pray, *transfigure me, Lord.*
When I feel sad, *transfigure me, Lord.*
When I feel tired, *transfigure me, Lord.*
When I cannot forgive, *transfigure me, Lord.*
When I cannot remember, *transfigure me, Lord.*
When I fear death, *transfigure me, Lord.*
When I feel alone, *transfigure me, Lord.*
When I forget your presence, *transfigure me, Lord.*
With the gift of time, *transfigure me, Lord.*
With the truth of love, *transfigure me, Lord.*
With each surrender, *transfigure me, Lord.*
In the comfort of family, *transfigure me, Lord.*
In the wisdom of years, *transfigure me, Lord.*
In the stillness and silence, *transfigure me, Lord.*
In my final breath, *transfigure me, Lord.*
In eternal life, *transfigure me, Lord.*
Amen.

PARENTS' PRAYER

The momentous task of parenting includes loving our children "just as they are" while simultaneously encouraging them to grow and change, to be their best selves. In this we imitate God, who loves us as we are but always calls us to something higher.

* * *

God our Father, you love us with the tender yet demanding love of a good parent. Your enduring love embraces us as we are; your creative love calls us forth to grow and change. Help us as parents to imitate your tenderness and love. May we embrace our children just as they are and encourage them forward to grow and change. Help us to guide them with consistency and compassion so they may grow up to be responsible and kind, joyful and faithful. Fill us with your Spirit of wisdom that we may act as faithful companions and able guides, leading them by the hand into the beauty of your presence, the happiness of your friendship, and the peace of your eternal embrace. Amen.

DEACON'S PRAYER (SERVANT'S PRAYER)

I wrote this prayer for deacons, but it can be prayed by anyone, of course. "Deacon" means "servant."

* * *

Lord Jesus Christ, Servant of all,
Send your Spirit upon me as I serve your Church.
Give me eyes to see the needs of your people.
Give me a discerning mind to know your truth.
Give me a generous spirit when I am tired but needed.
Give me a humble heart when my work goes unnoticed.
Give me peace of mind in obedience and service.
Give me health of body so I may serve with strength.
Make me fertile ground for your inspiration and love.
Comfort me when I question myself and my ministry.
Grant me grace as I age so I may share your wisdom.
Make my heart like yours so I may love your people.
Amen.

A PRAYER FOR YOUR MOM

Here's a prayer to the Holy Spirit that you can say for your mom. You could even say it for nine days and give her the gift of a novena. (If you don't remember what a novena is, ask your mom!) If your mom has entered eternal life, you can still pray it – the love you offer by saying it is not without value!

I based this prayer on St. Paul's description of the fruit of the Spirit: "love, joy, peace, patience, kindness, generosity, faithfulness, gentleness, self-control" (Gal. 5:22-23).

* * *

Come, Holy Spirit, pour into the heart of my mother the fullness of your life. Breathe into her your Spirit of love, enliven her with your joy, comfort her with your peace, impart to her your patience, and wrap her in your kindness. May she grow in your generosity, abide in your faithfulness and be renewed every day by your gentleness. Fill every emptiness in her heart and in her life with the power of your presence and the quiet of your healing love. As a mother bonds with her child, may my mother be bound to you in the depths of God's own heart, O Spirit of wisdom, Spirit of love, Spirit of Jesus, Spirit of joy. Amen.

NOTES

41854006R00064

Made in the USA
Middletown, DE
25 March 2017